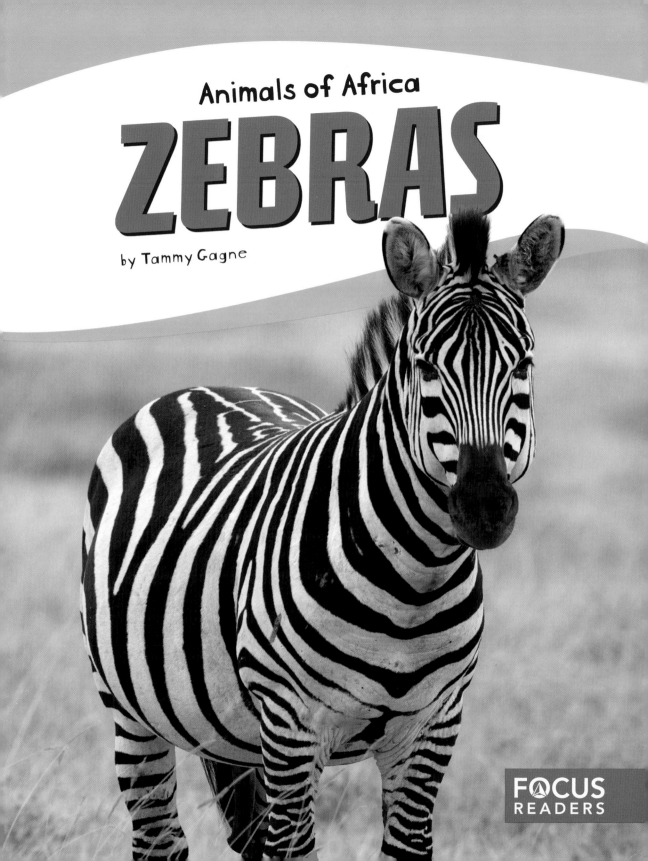

Animals of Africa
ZEBRAS

by Tammy Gagne

FOCUS READERS

FOCUS READERS

www.focusreaders.com

Focus Readers is distributed by North Star Editions:
sales@northstareditions.com | 888-417-0195

Produced for Focus Readers by Red Line Editorial.

Photographs ©: AndrejsJegorovs/iStockphoto, cover, 1; 1001slide/iStockphoto, 4–5, 9; Red Line Editorial, 6; GlobalP/iStockphoto, 10–11; WLDavies/iStockphoto, 12; mjf795/ iStockphoto, 15; Mari Swanepoel/Shutterstock Images, 16–17; prapassong/iStockphoto, 19, 29; chuvipro/iStockphoto, 20; MarieClaudeHH/iStockphoto, 22–23; Angela N Perryman/ Shutterstock Images, 24 (top); dawnn/iStockphoto, 24 (bottom right); urosr/iStockphoto, 24 (bottom left); Shak_Leinani/iStockphoto, 26

ISBN
978-1-63517-269-0 (hardcover)
978-1-63517-334-5 (paperback)
978-1-63517-464-9 (ebook pdf)
978-1-63517-399-4 (hosted ebook)

Library of Congress Control Number: 2017935120

Printed in the United States of America
Mankato, MN
June, 2017

About the Author

Tammy Gagne has written more than 150 books for adults and children. She resides in northern New England with her husband and son. One of her favorite pastimes is visiting schools to talk to kids about the writing process.

TABLE OF CONTENTS

CHAPTER 1

SURVIVING IN THE SAVANNA

The zebra herd gathers after a breakfast of grass and twigs. The late morning sun heats up the **savanna**. The zebras take a drink from the river. Then they will nap until the sun sets.

Zebras stop for a drink from the river.

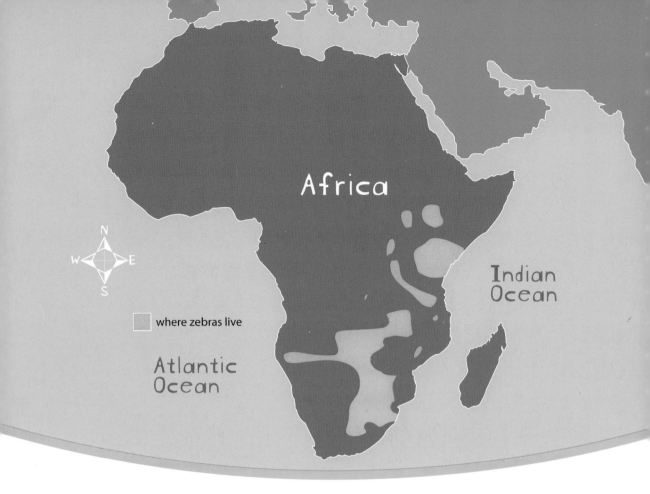

Africa

Indian Ocean

N
W E
S

where zebras live

Atlantic Ocean

Zebras live in parts of Africa.

Different types of zebras live in different areas. Plains zebras are the most common. They are named for the treeless grasslands where they live. Grevy's zebras also live in these flat regions. Mountain zebras are found in areas of higher ground.

Zebras live on open landscapes. They avoid forests where it is harder to escape **predators**. In open areas, they can try to run away.

If one zebra sees a cheetah in the distance, the zebra barks. It warns the others. The zebras move closer together. When facing a predator, zebras find strength in numbers.

MASSIVE MIGRATION

Many animals **migrate** when the seasons change. In the dry season, food and water become harder to find. The animals must move to where food and water are more plentiful. Zebras have the longest migrations of any land **mammal.**

Scientists study migration. They learn how much land the animals need. People can then protect this land. This helps the animals stay healthy.

Some zebras travel 300 miles (483 km) each year.

CHAPTER 2

STRIPES ON STRIPES

Most zebras stand 4.5 feet (1.4 m) tall at the shoulders. They weigh between 400 and 990 pounds (180 to 450 kg). Plains zebras are the smallest type. Grevy's zebras are the largest.

> **Zebras are members of the horse family.**

Zebras have black skin underneath their hair.

Male Grevy's zebras are larger than females. But most plains and mountain zebras are the same size.

Zebras have large heads. Their necks are muscular. They have long legs with hoofed feet. Zebras also have rough **manes**. They have **tasseled** tails, too.

A zebra's body is covered with short hair. Zebras have stripes. Each type of zebra has different colors and patterns. Most zebras have black stripes.

Some plains zebras have brown stripes. The Grevy's zebra's stripes are thinner than others. Mountain zebras have **vertical** stripes on their necks. They have **horizontal** stripes on their legs.

Most zebras do not have stripes over their entire bodies. Their bellies and the insides of their legs

FUN FACT

No two zebras' stripes are exactly alike. Each zebra has a different pattern.

A group of zebras face a lioness.

have no stripes. Both of these areas are covered with solid white hair.

CHAPTER 3

HIDING IN PLAIN SIGHT

Zebras have muscular legs. They use their legs to defend against predators. Their legs can deliver powerful kicks to predators such as hyenas or lions. They also help zebras outrun many predators.

Zebras can run up to 35 miles per hour (56 km/h).

Scientists do not know for sure why zebras have stripes. But they have many ideas. The stripes might act as **camouflage**. They help the animals blend into the grass. The patterns also make it hard for predators to see a single zebra in a herd. Stripes also cause problems

FUN FACT

Some scientists think zebras can recognize herd members by their stripe patterns.

PARTS OF A ZEBRA

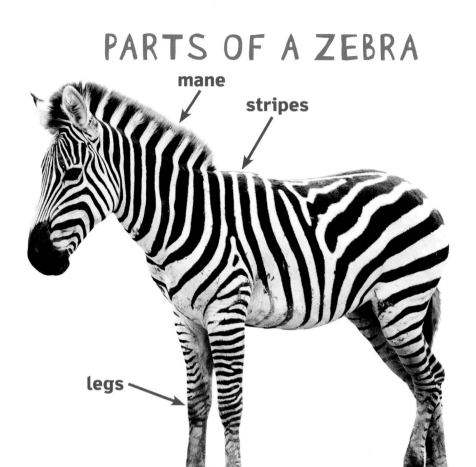

mane

stripes

legs

for predators that hunt in darkness.

Predators cannot tell how far away

the zebras are.

The stripes of many zebras blend together.

Zebras run in a zigzag pattern when chased. This makes it hard for predators to catch them.

Some scientists think stripes protect zebras from the hot sun. Others think stripes can help keep insects off the animal. Many insects seek out animals with fur that is only one color.

CHAPTER 4

STRENGTH IN NUMBERS

Zebras live together in groups called harems. Each harem includes a male zebra. He is called a stallion. A harem also includes several females and their young. Female zebras are called mares.

A stallion leads his harem.

ZEBRA LIFE CYCLE

Foals are born during the rainy season.

Zebras leave their mothers at approximately 3 years old.

Foals can walk soon after birth.

Babies are called foals. Harems often join together. They can include as many as 1,000 zebras.

Female zebras have one baby at a time. The mare keeps all the other zebras away from her offspring for two to three days. The foal learns to recognize its mother by sight, sound, and smell.

FUN FACT

Zebras can live for approximately 25 years.

 **Zebras graze on the savanna.**

Zebras bark when they see a

predator. This sound warns the

other harem members. If a zebra is attacked, the others come to its rescue. They form a circle around the injured animal. They drive away the predator.

Zebras eat mostly grass. They also eat leaves and shrubs. They sometimes eat tree bark and twigs. These materials are rough. But zebras have large teeth. They help the animals chew thick grass and tough stems.

FOCUS ON
ZEBRAS

Write your answers on a separate piece of paper.

1. Write a letter to a friend describing what you learned about a zebra's diet.

2. Which trait do you think best helps zebras avoid predators? Why?

3. Which type of zebra has thin stripes?
   A. plains zebra
   B. Grevy's zebra
   C. mountain zebra

4. What might happen if a zebra wanders off from its harem?
   A. It would have trouble finding food.
   B. Its harem would reject it when it tried to return.
   C. A predator would be able to catch it more easily.

5. What does **plains** mean in this book?

Plains zebras are the most common. They are named for the treeless grasslands where they live.

    A. flat land with few tall plants

    B. steep, mountainous regions

    C. deep valleys

6. What does **offspring** mean in this book?

Female zebras have one baby at a time. The mare keeps all the other zebras away from her **offspring** *for two to three days.*

    A. an animal's parents

    B. an animal's brothers and sisters

    C. an animal's young

Answer key on page 32.

GLOSSARY

camouflage
Colors that make an animal difficult to see in the area around it.

horizontal
Arranged in a side-to-side pattern.

mammal
An animal that gives birth to live babies, has fur or hair, and produces milk.

manes
The hair that grows on the necks of some animals.

migrate
To move from one region to another at the change of the seasons.

predators
Animals that hunt other animals for food.

savanna
A grassland with few or no trees.

tasseled
Resembles something bound at one end and falling freely at the other.

vertical
Arranged in an up-and-down pattern.

TO LEARN MORE

BOOKS

Carmichael, L. E. *Zebra Migration*. North Mankato, MN: The Child's World, 2012.

Higgins, Melissa. *Grassland Ecosystems*. Mankato, MN: Abdo Publishing, 2016.

Spelman, Lucy. *Animal Encyclopedia*. Washington, DC: National Geographic Kids, 2012.

NOTE TO EDUCATORS

Visit **www.focusreaders.com** to find lesson plans, activities, links, and other resources related to this title.

INDEX

Answer Key: 1. Answers will vary; **2.** Answers will vary; **3.** B; **4.** C; **5.** A; **6.** C